Shout If You Want Me To Sing

Imelda Maguire

SUMMER PALACE PRESS

First published in 2004 by

Summer Palace Press
Cladnageeragh, Kilbeg, Kilcar, County Donegal, Ireland

Printed by Nicholson & Bass Ltd.

A catalogue record for this book is available
from the British Library

ISBN   0   9544752   6   7

This book is printed on elemental chlorine-free paper

for
my mother and father, Mary and Tom Maguire,
who sang to me
and
my son, Gavin,
who is his own song,
music to my ears.

Acknowledgments

Some of the poems in this book have previously appeared in:

Beyond the Rubicon (Covehill Press, 1999); *A Deeper Light* (Glass Apple Writers, 2002); *Eleven Ways to Kiss the Ground* (CD, Errigal Writers, 2001); *The SHOp* (2004).

Biographical Note

Imelda Maguire was born in Kildare. She grew up in Limerick, spent sixteen years in Sligo, and has lived, since 1995, in Donegal. She is a member of two Letterkenny-based writers' groups: Errigal Writers and Glass Apple Writers. She was overall winner of the 1999 Athlone Poetry Competition. She took part in Poetry Ireland Introductions Series 2002, and has read her work at Earagail Arts Festival, in the Irish Writers Centre and in Derry's Verbal Arts Centre. She tutors and facilitates Creative Writing groups throughout County Donegal.

CONTENTS

Origins

I come from a bog-cotton,
hawk-cry, flat, plain place;
from a father who was
a motherless boy.
I come from a factory-chimney,
mouth-of-the-river city;
from a line of strong, proud
women, good with their hands;
from a mother who was
eldest of eight,
working at twelve,
keeping house for families
where children older than she
were cosseted and sent to school.

I come from someplace
between the cold that called
for greatcoats piled on the bed
and the white-hot heat of
a Saturday night range;
somewhere between the piety
of nightly rosary and the radical
words of my father, berating the clergy
who persecuted the last few
Limerick Jews.

I come from times that were changing
and carry a residue of times
that never will.

The Forbidden Room

And when Nana was left alone
after my maiden aunt died,
they sent me to live with her,
to be there at nights, at least.

Mine was the small room
upstairs, the one without a wardrobe.
My clothes gradually found their way
over the back of the chair,
slunk to the floor,
pooled behind the door;
thoughts of lifting and folding
sullenly banished. I wanted
that room with the pink carpet,
armchair, double wardrobe, view
of the garden, quilted stool
at the dressing-table, and once
I went and did my homework there.

I didn't know that Nana knew until
Saturday, when Mother came
to take me home, and Cousin
Caroline went to stay,
so Nana wouldn't be alone.

Lost and Found

Things I have lost:
>A few umbrellas. I no longer carry one.
>A silver ring – three strands plaited, a pretty thing,
>>my very first.
>A poem sent to me by my friend.
>Some memories. Now, I don't know which ones they were.

And found:
>On Spiddal beach, among the stones, a pendant,
>>no chain attached, a fairy charm.
>Late at night, a bunch of carnations, fresh,
>>lying in the middle of our street.
>In Strandhill, on my loneliest day, a pebble
>>with the imprint of a long-gone sea shell.

Mother

The things I've learnt from you
may not be those skills usually
passed from mother to daughter.
I still can't bake a loaf of bread
or manage to get every room
tidied in one day.

But I can take pleasure in my garden,
stroll around and inventory the plants
like you used to.
Remember calling us all down
to show us a bleeding heart,
or your Calvary plant?

Whenever I pile the contents of a room
in the hallway, intent
on doing a proper clear-out,
I think of you.
You'd do that too, and then
a shaft of sunlight
or chorus of birdsong
would draw you outdoors.
There we'd find you
when we came in from school,
swinging on the back-garden swing,
face up to the sunshine,
whistling with the blackbird.

You drove us mad with your vagaries.
You taught me there's never a time
to stop asking questions.
Look at you.
Seventy, and still at it.

In Bengal Terrace

The day is a flagpole in the middle of the year,
between my birthdays.
I am nine-and-a-half today,
and my pigtails are heavy.

Auntie Imelda's paper says the date is June 1st.
She reads, and I lick my ice-cream slowly.
We sit on the white garden seat.
Nana paints it every year in May –
a fresh coat, before it's needed.

In one month I will have holidays from school
and from piano lessons, but I will still come
on Tuesdays and Fridays to Nana's house
to visit and have pineapple juice,
go to the shop for messages – milk in the can
and ice-cream wafers.
I am nine-and-a-half and the summer will be long.

A bugle call fills the garden,
echoes up the terrace – long notes,
three repeated. I know it, I know that call.
They play it at soldiers' funerals
in the cemetery across the road.
When soldiers, like my grandfather, die,
they sound the last post.

When my grandfather died,
one of his pals came at night,
stood at the gate of the house,
and sang that song, so my mother said.
I never heard it sung – only played on the bugle.

Soon the loud bang, loud guns, loud noise
will follow, three volleys over the grave,
to say *He was a soldier,*
and the smell will wander over the high wall
to the garden where we're sitting.
I am nine-and-a-half when I realise
it isn't only soldiers who die.

Auntie Imelda, tossing the newspaper,
pink lips, pink nails, will die.
Nana, in the kitchen peeling potatoes, will die.
I, nine-and-a-half, with heavy pigtails
and beginning-to-tan feet,
one day, one day, I will die.

Unscheduled Stop

The train halts on the slope
of the mountain, on the way up,
with the screech of wheel on rail.
We sit in the heat. Passengers crane
out windows to see what's ahead.
       Beside me, just beyond the tracks,
       an almond grove: straw-strewn earth;
       twisted trees, leaves crisped to the turn
       of the season.
       The almonds are held in a hairy cup.
       I never knew that,
       never saw one growing before.
       If I reach out my hand now,
       I could touch that tree.
The woman in the gold-spangled blouse
pesters her husband to go and find out
the cause of this delay.
Men step down beside the train
for a smoke. A local workman
reads about the assassination attempt
on an election candidate.
       If I reach out my arm,
       I could touch that tree.
       I could prise that precious nut
       from its tight carapace.
A girl applies another layer of sun cream,
a child gathers discarded brochures.
A whistle up ahead –
passengers reclaim their seats.
We move on.
       I have not touched the almond tree.

Things About You

I like to tell people these things about you:

you bought yourself a car for your fiftieth birthday,
before you even knew how to drive.

One Sunday you brought home fruit, sweets, biscuits,
told us it was Children's Day – and that was dinner.

You used to sit for hours on the back garden swing,
soaking up the garden, soaking it all up.

You grew peas and let us eat them
right out of the pod – never cooked any.

Once, on a Monday, you sent the boys to school,
put Aileen and me in the car, and we went to Killarney.

You went to charismatic meetings
until people started to speak in tongues.

Now you see your kitchen window-box
for the first time, every time you go into the room,

and you say,
Just look at those lovely pansies.

Confession

Woolworths, Bolgers, Todds
lay out their stalls.
Everything you need to be a woman.
Reds and pinks and peachy shades
for lips – *Catch that man,*
Catch that boy.
We have all the tools right here.

I am thirteen.
Stashed at the back of my wardrobe:
three copies of *Jackie*, a *Romeo*;
a palette of greens;
a palette of blues;
a little tub of gunmetal grey
for eyes.

Best days are Saturdays,
mid-afternoon, especially
if the countrywomen are around.
They ask questions, distract
the saleswomen, who know,
when they see us,
or think they know.

Holy Mary, Mother of God.
I light candles, pray for my sins,
but neglect to put my penny
in the box beneath the candles.
Sin on sin. I promise myself
to put it right. Next time
I will put it right.

Next time we're in town
Roches has a sale.
Busy in every department.
I come home
with four embroidery silks,
a brown leather purse, quite small,
and lipstick – scarlet, scarlet, scarlet –
a shade I've never worn.

Advice for George

The past hurts, George, but sing and be merry.
Andrei Voznesensky

We don't want to hear about the hurts.
And we don't want to hear about the past, George,
or the weapon you made of your pain –
how you gouged your own heart out.
What were you thinking of?

Could you not have had a drink, George?
or found yourself a woman,
            or a man, come to that?
We're very open-minded here.

Why do you keep going back to it, George?
Do you think there's a cure in the depths
            of that wound?
Do you think you can empty it,
drain it enough
to let it heal, George?

What are you thinking of, George,
carrying your past around in an open box,
letting it spill at our feet as you walk?

Fix the lid tight, George.
Stand up on that box of yours.
Fill your lungs.
Get ready to sing.

A Life in Green

Make it green, my life –
all the shades and smells of it.

Curragh-smooth
and back-field secret,
Hanly's-field-wild.

Give it the green
of the Shannon's tidal places,
and the rushes on Cleeve's bank.

Add all the green of Poor Man's Kilkee –
grass stubble, scuffed earth
where teenage feet kick and pick.

Put in front-garden cabbage,
and pea-plant green.

Take the green fingers
of new leaves on conker trees
behind the asylum walls.

Add the bitter green of acid in the heart.
A gap-toothed girl
with my first love.

Spread to the tans and duns
overlaid with moss
on a mountain's slope.

Ben Bulben's hundred colours,
hundred lights, and Hazelwood's green,
Lough Gill green,

the greens of freedom,
and the green of new life growing,
pressure beneath my ribs,

filling me all through Spring – my son,
my greensummer baby.

Keep trails and traces of green promise
everywhere, green buds and shoots.
Green in the flame of a dying fire.

Blades

Summer days,
I am a child, hiding
in feathery, finger-cutting
grass two feet high,
behind the pear trees,
behind the berry patch,
sucking nectar from pink clover.

Teenage times,
two tuppenny pieces
for the bus home alone,
chewing on stalks,
waiting to be noticed,
teeth gone green with grass,
not knowing,
sitting on a green space
near the river.

Now the grass is mine,
lawn front and back.
A man comes every ten days
to keep it neat,
keep the daisies down,
keep the clover in check.

Gabriel's Children

after Luka Bloom

We come to now, our forties,
    and suddenly, angels matter again.
    Our children are the cynics
    and we look where we can for guardians.

I hear you call *Gabriel*, and the name
    is beautiful to me; a pale trace
    of wings on the edge of my vision;
    an intimation of light in the air.

Long ago, when I first knew you,
    between rounds of lectures and coffee-shop,
    were we looking for angels then?
    Searching without knowing the name?
    Were we always Gabriel's children?

Apology

I wronged you,
William Carlos Williams,
thinking you were all
red wheelbarrows
and white chickens.

Doc, I bin lookin' for you, indeed.
I didn't know you had
war cries in you,
didn't know you were
more than a sugar-pill poet.

Hey Doc,
glad I found you.
How about some cool sweet plums?
This is just to say
Sorry.

Grown Up

I take pepper on almost everything;
drink coffee or tea;
watch TV into the small hours;
pass toyshops without a glance;
buy bargain packs of cotton-rich socks
and think, *That was a good day's shopping.*

In parks, I look for a free bench;
haven't set a naked foot on naked grass in years;
I eat ice-cream in little spoonfuls;
check doors and windows at night;
stretch a good book over a week;
reach for the pepper to add some flavour.

Singland Road

Childhood has a moveable frame
   shaped like a tadpole cloud
      or a crayoned sun, or a
Boo! jumping at me
   with the sting of a nettle,
      the shock of slipping
         into a chilled stream
            on the hunt for pinkies in Singland
            and the boys' gang laughing.
I want to run away,
   to hide in the ancient salleys
      in the green-red gloom of a den
         beyond the railway line
            forgotten now by everyone,
            stay hidden forever,
hoping someone will come and find me soon.

Rock Pools

... and in REFERENCE,
where dictionaries line up
waiting to spill meaning
into my world,
I find the Top Ten of Everything.

I flick: *Fastest Flying Insects,*
        Most Bombed Areas of Europe,
        Most Expensive Films Ever Made.

Between page 110 – *Tallest Standing Statues:*
Crazy Horse, all those Buddhas –
and page 111 – *Largest Paintings in the Louvre:*
battles; rivers; all those Napoleons –
someone's left a snapshot,
black and white,
a summer picture, and on the back
in purpling ink, *Cousins 1963.*

The children are crouched at a rockpool:
two girls in gingham shirts
– the older one has a net –
a boy with a bucket.
The toddler, pudgy legs,
plump cheeks under a sun-bonnet,
is between the knees of a grandad,
a gaunt man, shirt open at the neck,
braces holding up Sunday trousers.
His eyes are deep in caverns,
fingers lie loose on the boy's shoulder
like strips of bleached bladderwrack.

The children grin into the lens.
The man's eyes won't meet the camera,
won't meet the eyes behind it.
They won't meet mine, but I meet

my
       Top Ten Cousin Memories,
       Top Ten Summer-in-Kilkee Days,
       Top Ten Dying Grandad Pictures.

Cuttings

My mother hardly ever left a garden
without a slip or two discreetly detached
from a coveted plant.

The day we first visited the convent
I prayed no nun would ever pass our garden
and know that I lived there.

I sat mute, mortified,
while four plump twigs of hebe
nestled in my mother's handbag.

I never filch a plant myself,
am generous with cuttings already rooted,
potted up, ready to go.

But my friends need only watch for the times
my ears prick up at some slant of their tales,
when I glance at a picture from their world,

scraps stored in a mental notebook,
borrowed without permission –
slips of other people's lives.

Thorn Road – October

Blue in the sheen on a bellowing
black cow's haunch;
purple-blue splash of sloes
on an arching branch;
indigo berries hold tight to brambles.
Wingtip flash of a startled crow – blue;
dust film on underside of beech leaves – blue;
roadside spruce all puffed up in a winter coat,
soft green tinged with turquoise blue;
the Swilly, gunmetal watered-silk.
No blue in the expected places,
but touching the world, faintly, lightly,
colouring the air – blue.

Visit

for Paula Meehan

That poem was only ever passing through.
I knew when it said *OK* grudgingly to a cup of tea,
but wouldn't take a sandwich, however hard I pressed,
said it was watching the figure, being careful.

I said, *Ah sure, I know, but I have home-made apple-tart.*
Will you have some of that?
And the poem said, *No. It smells lovely, but no,*
just sat on the edge of the chair,
coat unbuttoned, not letting me take it,
saying *No, thanks, I'll leave it on. I won't stay long.*

I knew I'd never coax it into ease,
into telling me a secret or a story,
into shaking the hair back and laughing.

To spare my dignity, and because the poem
was polite too, I said, *Well, it was very good*
of you to drop by, as the poem stood up,
and I really hope you'll call again some day
when you have more time.

Then I put flowers in the guest room
in case tomorrow or the next day,
another poem happened along,
one with time on its hands,
in the mood for a chat.

Moving – 15th August, 1998

My task is to ferry small things
 – boxes, plants, pictures –
leave the furniture
for the men with the van.

In the car between my sister's new house
and the flat she's leaving
I hear snatches of news:
a bomb, up North.

I tell them when I come in
with kettle and iron.
No one has tuned in the TV.
I go again, to fetch ferns and ficus.

It might be bad. Reports of fatalities.
Confirmed. When I return,
it's all still so unclear.
There may be up to thirteen dead.

What about the ceasefire? Children?
Saturday afternoon, summer. Isn't this a Holy Day?
I gather bags of sheets and towels,
a box of framed photos, a collection of teapots.

In the new house, they are sitting on the floor,
pictures on the TV now. Mayhem.
Chaos. Numbers still not known.
But there may be more than thirteen dead.
There may be more.

Dream

In the soft mud of sleep:

the number fourteen;
a dinner-setting, cream china
with a gold rim;
one wing of an orange butterfly;
the coiled shell of a garden snail.

Morning offers no translation.

Splinters

Splinters were my father's job.
He had the magic of removing them
without a trace of pain.
He would lull me to sleep,
even with a fiery throbbing finger,
and only then he'd set to work
with a tiny needle;
prise skin open just enough
to reach the thorn or sliver
of wood; ease it from my flesh.
And in the morning, only a pinprick
to remind me
of last night's misery.

But his eye is not keen enough,
needle not fine enough
for the barbs
that burrow straight through,
working their silent way
to the core,
lodging there.
Scar tissue still throbs
at an unexpected touch,
burns at a word,
sends ghost pain shooting,
makes me long
for a visit in the night
from some other spirit-wizard
to carry away this sting.

Wasp

This is what a wasp looks like
when it's dead.
It looks like a living wasp
but it doesn't move.
The wings are still
translucent onion-skin traceries
shaped like sycamore seed.

This is what a wasp sounds like
when it's dead. Nothing.
The angry buzz that gathered
every summer
under Nana's kitchen window – gone.
The wasp lies curled,
humbled, and makes no noise.

This is what a wasp feels like
when it's dead. Nothing.
It feels like nothing –
so light it's just
a thumbnail-sized
black-and-yellow
hologram of an angry beast.
Filament-antennae
search empty air
for the source of threat.
Stripes warn
Do not touch,
Do not taste.

Body curled into defence
or attack. The sting,
the nib lifting to pierce.
The head bowed;
upper body rolled
into a peppercorn-shaped ball
covered with a fine black fuzz.

Not what a living wasp
looks like.
Not at all.

Insomnia

The night-time clock
shears seconds off my sleep.
Shreds of its fabric lie
around me while I toss.
The snick-snick sound
echoing in my tired head
pounds through the pillow,
drives me up to seek
peace in the kitchen.

Three in the morning,
the dog wags a tired tail,
stretches, settles and returns
to her sleep, while I sit,
wait for silence,
wanting rest. The kitchen clock
snips every second of this time.
Jagged pinked strips
flutter in the air. At the window,
surprised moths.

How to Build a Salamander
after Gaudi

You'll need the kind of wife who shouts a lot,
stamps her feet and throws things – pots,
plates, all the crockery piled on the table.

Better yet, a mistress or two girlfriends – lots
of women smashing all around them. Give them
reason to. It's all in the cause of art.

When they leave, as they will, gather the bits.
Sweep all the broken pieces into piles. Save them
somewhere out of sight until the time is right.

Then – you'll know just when – climb to the roof
of a house with odd windows, misshapen doors.
Sleep in the sun until your brain feels fried.

When it seems as if the plane trees below are saying
Jump; when it seems that the sky has blue dragons
painted on blue that only you can see,

call the boy, fill a barrow with your hoard – with
plaster, wine, all the stuff essential to the work.
Yellow, mustard, lemon, tan, terra, all blues,

all greens – a hundred shades, product of years
of anger, product of fury and a name gone to mud.
Pebbles – smooth, rounded, black, cream, polished, brown.

Where the park will be, sit and wait
until an eye blinks before you. Catch it.
Place one cobalt shard right there, and wait.

The rippling of skin becomes a frantic challenge
to capture – work fast, grab pieces, bleeding fingers
placing waves and rivulets of colour on the beast,

the beast that calls you – only you – to give it life.
Under your hand, a heart beats. Under your hand
a quick tongue flicks, a cold eye glimmers.

Ashore

Days cruise in secret and lie in ambush …
                    Pablo Neruda

Whenever I think, *That's that. The past is done,*
those days that haven't got the message yet
sail right back in, come floating
up the undammed river of my life, flags waving,
cannons pointing into now, my present.

There they are, letting down their anchors,
taking on provisions, settling in for a long stay,
time ashore for the crew and passengers.

There they are, wandering the streets of my life,
window-shopping. Oh, that one is lifting goods
without apology, without payment.
And her, the skinny bitch, just sits in a chair
at the front of my life and waits for me to ask,
Well, what did you forget to tell me?

At the window, little girls lined up
tracing names in the dust.
Always the same names.
Always the same faces.

Crossing

That duck
on the slip-road leaving Longford:
her two berry-bright eyes
when she emerged from the hedge;
her *here-I-come* bill
when she started across the rain-slick road;
her five little waddling young,
curious, quick, tripping after her.

Her faith, their trust.
I stop the car
and in me
something brightens,
something lifts.

A Recollection of Maghery Beach, 20 September, 2001

Through the afternoon we sit, encircled,
and the healing is in *I remember ...*
I wonder ... I thought ... I was thinking ...
and the healing is in silence,
and the healing is in gathering,
neighbours coming in,
coming together ...

Late evening, I stroll the beach.
The air is filled with salt and gulls' cries.
To the west the sky takes light,
flares up, flames out over water,
rock and land.
What slips underfoot is pebbles
smoothed over years.
What I seek is the perfect stone,
the one that fits a hand,
the shape of a heart.

Over there, beyond the ocean
where the sun has gone,
another fire, other searchers seeking
signs of life. There the air is filled
with dust and pain, there at Ground Zero,
just across the way, in the next place west
of Maghery beach,
just beyond the sunset, just across there.

Déjà-vû
for Kerry Hardie and Ellen Hinsey

Like now, when you read a poem
about a dying friend
and his lover's way of carrying him
from bed to window,
something in me said: *Yes, I know*
and slipped away again.

And that poem about not having time,
no longer waiting for flowers
but enjoying the leaves, reminds me
that in these last months
Esther is still gathering flat smooth stones
for her garden, has pruned her wisteria.

Something there is connected too.
Under the surface these pictures
have the same lines,
the same pale shades.

Sadrat'ul-Muntahà (Tree of Life)

My thoughts are restless evening rooks,
circling, wheeling,
coming to rest only in the tree of you.

You are every tree the earth
has ever cast from her womb,
calling me to rest a cheek on warm bark.

I wake, a sweet taste of green in my mouth.
You are the one tree
that cast five seeds.

Now, half-way through July
everyone bemoans this grey dullness;
because this year we did not dance

in midsummer's light,
because we lit no bonfire,
darkness will fall earlier.

The lazy moth of morning
hiding from the light, seeking darkness.
I crumble it in my fingers,
rub its silver on my cheeks.

When all five seeds
have taken to the soil,
then will there be a blossoming.

The chanting flowers
will sing the song of that one tree.
That Tree of Life
will call me, soothe me, lull me to sleep,
black wings folded against the night.

Brief Lines from Falcarragh

for Cathal Ó Searcaigh

a cloud chases
ripples of light
along the mountain's flank

drift of turfsmoke
over low pasture
cattle home for milking

the bellowing cow
mist moves
through the townland

this cold evening
the silence
on your breath

frayed rope
on the old sycamore
by the gable

in moonlight
the long lane
points skyward

the icy night
your footsteps
and the taste of cloves

country road
an old man
salutes an empty house

in the morning
dew-washed leaves
on red-lipped hawthorn

Catalogue

Woman in shades of purple
Self-portrait as a body of water
Tree with one fruit
Woman with squirrel's eyes
Self-portrait with pen and paper
Woman with yellow aura
Impression – before autumn
Nude in locked bathroom
Woman with frail wings
Untitled – Not for sale.

After Spring Break – Where Colours Go

The house holds its breath,
and when I come back in
after a fortnight's absence,
it exhales dead air,
relieved I am the same.
Life will go on as normal.

The orange lilies I'd forgotten
have shed their petals –
colour seeped away,
bled onto the carpet.
Now their grey traces
must be peeled up off the floor.

I wish I could surround myself
tonight with oleander, hibiscus,
jacaranda, bougainvillea –
bright and clear,
lush and full of Spain.

London, September '97

London is a dangerous place
where Jack the Ripper stalked
and junkies roam, and you might be
alone
among ten million people.
And the Underground
no place for a girl
or a woman alone.
I've known it all my life.

But this year, as I'm nearing forty,
and on my fifth visit,
and now that I believe in empowerment,
feeling the fear and doing it anyway,
I strike out alone,
my daily travel-pass safely tucked
   in my securely held
      strap-across-my-chest
         shoulder-bag,
money hidden in jeans pocket,
and some to spare, secreted elsewhere.
I have an adventure;
discover, all on my own,
a wonderland, a marvel
– Kew Gardens –
last stop before Richmond, District Line.
I find lemon trees, jasmine,
lotus-flower, papyrus.

Bravely and fearlessly
I return,
carrier bags bulging
bargain packs of spring bulbs.
I sashay along the platform
for the Victoria Line,
Northbound.

Six Ways to Kneel and Kiss the Ground

There are a hundred ways to kneel and kiss the ground ...
Rumi

Stand stock-still, watch a red admiral sail
beyond your garden and your neighbours.

Place your palm on the warm bark of a maple,
pat it, pet it; if you're brave, put your face
against the smooth grain of it; wrap your arms
tight around the trunk. Hug.

Brush your nose in the shampooed silk
of a three-year-old's storytime head.

Breathe air flowing in from the sea.

Breathe air flowing down from the mountain.

Lie on summer grass; roll over;
feel the blades on your cheek;
place your lips on the earth;
kiss.

This Day: 4 July, 2002, Bantry

Now they are tossing the papers,
trying to shake the best bits of news
onto the table, to rattle the rest of the story
out like the last embers from the range.

It doesn't work like that! I want to say.
It isn't like Hampton Court Flower Show either –
model gardens made in six days, dismantled in one,
at the end of the second glorious week.

You think a recipe is all you need – for
beans on toast, a garden, the perfect war
or air-strike. Show me the pictures now. Where
are the bodies? Where is the blood?

Outside, a saint whose name escapes me
stretches bronze arms to the sea –
a call for calm or a beckoning.
Here, tell me the news. Tell me.

How the World Began

on hearing the Australian legend of Crying Baby

The sky is sucking sparks
from the fire in great gulps.
It draws them up, replaces
hidden stars with quick brightness.

Thompson Yulidjirri draws with a thin finger
in smoothed sand. The story, as he speaks,
traces the times and journeys from
dreamtime to storytime, to here, to now.

Does he notice that trees, water, sky,
all bend to the tale, all come to the edge
of the clearing he makes, like shy creatures?
That the rain waits until he's silent
before it falls?

Glimmer

I caught a glimmer of you on the wet walls,
a glimpse, a shine,
a shape that might be you,
there, moving and liquid, slipping away.

Nothing I could hold on to,
nothing I could say for sure *is*:
it must have been hope
made me think it was you.

Longing made that flicker
take on your shape;
the part of me that won't say *gone*
or *end* or *finish*

that glanced, saw a glimmering light
and claimed it: said *It must be you.*
And now the sun is rising,
damp walls soaking in heat,

drying out,
and your shape is leaving,
no longer mine,
no longer there.

Safety Strategies

The thistle makes each leaf a weapon,
curled and twisted,
spines facing every direction;
a ring-fortress
of glaucous warning;
and her head, the glorious pompom,
purple feathering that calls the bees,
held high above its stalk
on a collar of tight leather scales.

The buttercup
creeps up to the thistlepatch,
snuggles in, weaves her way surely
among those standing sentries,
tosses a glad head,
spreads out under the eye
of vigilant thistles,
safe in their great-auntish shadow.

What an orchid at the bog's edge does:
pretends to be clover; pretends to be heather;
displays the same shades – pink paling to cream,
or veering to mauve. She stays low to the ground
close to a flowing stream
where passing animals seek water,
not grazing.
But when she catches my eye
I kneel to the frailty and dogged clinging
of her, that speckled perfection
ranged on a tiny spire,
each open spotted throat.

Verses from a Summer

I was a pale lilac blossom,
a blue tree,
a whistle in the evening,

but you are a purple mountain,
your slopes all shifting shale,
my worn shoe slipping.

I dreamt I lived in a wide, high space,
not finished, all open, full of air
and pale, pale hangings,

but I know I will be a long time
prising rust-brown nails from the walls
of the rooms I still inhabit.

The Mourner

I have glimpsed her in my midnight window,
that silent sister of my soul,
hoarder of my unremembered dreams.
Still weeping all the tears I've put behind me,
she moves beside me through my days,
hauling losses with her. She picks through
salvaged pains, endlessly turning
them in her palms, reminding herself
of hurts and all the howling purple rage
that I have abandoned.

I have seen her eyes,
those winter pools of grief.
She will not loose her hold,
guardian of sobs and sighs,
of every part-mourned loss.
She is patient, and sure the time
will come when she is given voice,
keeper of my heart,
curator of dreams
that will not come to pass.

Arrival

Out of the turf-smoke grey mist
on Scalp mountain,
a streak-stream of silver
turns to white.

Haydn's *Surprise* an accident
on the radio
to match the moment;
I stop the car.

From the hard shoulder
I watch their wild-wonder descent
to that unerring point.
Their certainty that *now* is here,
these whooper swans' October arrival,
this Fall.

In Crêpe Paper

Because there was a rush of *Yes*
into the mind of the teacher and
because the *Yes* became a sound,

Yes, she said, *Yes*, to the child at last,
because he finally heard the *Yes*,
he carried it home like a bright yellow flower,

a big one with petals made of sunlight
to a mother who was waiting for a *Yes*,
because the word was carried in

in the mouth of her heartchild, that *Yes*
became the answer, the chant, the only
word in her day-long litany.

Yes, Yes, Yes

Sorrow Is a Deep, Deep Well

full of undrinkable water.
She is impenetrable,
a stout wall of stone
around the heart.

Sorrow is cold,
chilled to the bone,
unmoving, paralysed.

Sorrow holds tight,
wraps herself
into sinew and muscle,
wends her way through
vein and artery,
winds into the whorls
around the corpus callosum.

Sorrow holds herself
until the first tear
slips its salt way
down a cheek,
until the first sound,
the primeval wail,
keening of the soul,
seeps between the rocks
of the heart's wall.

Song of Purple

I am night-sky, mountain, heather;
the sea in its deepest places,
the rocks that it hides;
the colour taken on by periwinkles
in their hidden crevices.

I am crocus, iris,
lilac wants to be me,
rhododendrons crave my depth.
I am blue eyes darkening, the colour of bruises.
I am the land before storms,
the colour in the trees as they lose their last leaves.

I am the lofty colour that still clings to earth in its lowest places:
the steep cleft between rocks – look, not black, but purple;
when you dig the earth you think is brown look, look for me.
You'll find me there in the crumbled shale of earth's own surface.

I am the colour in the depth of the fire,
at the core of its heat – watch for the purple flame, feel its power.
I am in the sheen of a raven's wing, the spot on a salmon's back,
in the deep woodland flowers,
tiny ones that only scent the air
at certain times, from secret half-seen places
hidden in the purple shadow of last year's leaf-mould.

The Reckless Sleeper

after Ren Magritte

He sleeps in snatches –
moments, seconds only between calls,
and then he may spend hours bargaining
before he'll make the trade:
it isn't every symbol he'll accept
in return for these, the choice of dreamers.
You'll never know what it would take
to buy that bird:
maybe three golden cups;
maybe an ear;
and that apple can only be exchanged
for a certain flower
at a certain stage of growth.
Ah, very few will find themselves
standing with the necessary goods,
and the word – never written –
that will call the keeper of dreams
from his sleep
to make the deal.

Here. See the candle.
You'd think if your dream had a lamp
or a star or a bright sun
you'd qualify for that,
but Jarmid's code dictates
something bitten or bleeding
as the only acceptable substitute.
He'll send the supplicant away,
their lamp quenched,
their star swirling into blackness
to face cold sweat,
a thumping heart
in their waking.

Lines Found in Bantry, July 2003

My mother always told me that
it would get harder the older I got.

I only know as much as the next person
about death.

We'll play it by ear, though,
see how it goes.

Home calls, but if you have an angel
to take you by the hand
it's a great deal easier.

When a voice spoke in my head
and said, *That's enough*, it was,
so I stopped.